AF408415

FROM ME TO ME

Stephania Monroy

Every day I say a cheer full of nice words from me to me.

I AM KIND
I AM PRETTY
I AM SMART

When I wake up or before I sleep,
these kind words I will repeat.

GOOD NIGHT!

Each day I add a new affirmation to my jar.
It makes my heart dance like a bright star.

I AM...
BEAUTIFUL
KIND
SMART

Monday, I say "Thank you for this day."

Tuesday, I say "I love myself."

Wednesday, I say "I can do amazing things today."

I CAN

Thursday, I say "I am loved", and I give myself a hug.

Friday, I say "I am smart and important."

Saturday, I say "I am unique; nobody else looks like me."

And lastly, Sunday, I say "I am a star,
and I am perfect the way I am."

One last phrase I must think.

My own nice words, from me to me.

To every grown-up reading this book with their little ones, I hope it reminds you to be kind to yourself and mindful of the words you tell yourself each day.

Para papá y mamá que me dieron todo, Gracias.

Love,
Stephania Monroy

FROM ME TO ME

COPYRIGHT © 2024 BY STEPHANIA MONROY

ALL RIGHTS RESERVED. NO PART OF THIS PUBLICATION MAY BE REPRODUCED, DISTRIBUTED, OR TRANSMITTED IN ANY FORM OR BY ANY MEANS, INCLUDING PHOTOCOPYING, RECORDING, OR OTHER ELECTRONIC OR MECHANICAL METHODS, WITHOUT THE PRIOR WRITTEN PERMISSION OF STEPHANIA MONROY, EXCEPT IN THE CASE OF BRIEF QUOTATIONS EMBODIED IN CRITICAL REVIEWS AND CERTAIN OTHER NONCOMMERCIAL USES PERMITTED BY COPYRIGHT LAW.

FOR INQUIRIES OR PERMISSIONS, PLEASE CONTACT THE AUTHOR: STEPHANIA MONROY @CAMILOADVENTURESBOOK

FIRST EDITION PUBLISHED 2024

www.ingramcontent.com/pod-product-compliance
Lightning Source LLC
Chambersburg PA
CBHW041938110726

48010CB00003B/145